NIGHT RADIO

THE AGHA SHAHID ALI PRIZE IN POETRY

NIGHT RADIO ⋮ KIM YOUNG

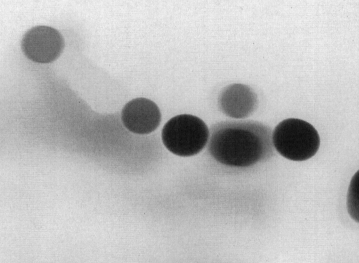

THE UNIVERSITY OF UTAH PRESS

*Salt Lake City*

AGHA SHAHID ALI

PRIZE IN POETRY

The Agha Shahid Ali Prize in Poetry
*Series Editor:* Katharine Coles
*Advisory Editor:* Jacqueline Osherow

The Defiance House Man colophon is a registered trademark of the
University of Utah Press. It is based on a four-foot-tall Ancient
Puebloan pictograph (late PIII) near Glen Canyon, Utah.

19 18 17 16 15      2 3 4 5 6

Library of Congress Cataloging-in-Publication Data
Young, Kim, 1975-
  Night radio / Kim Young.
      p. cm.
  isbn 978-1-60781-206-7 (ebook)
  I. Title.
  PS3625.O96546N54 2012
  811'.6—dc23

                                          2012021494

# CONTENTS

## 3 ¦ LATCHKEY

Imagine this as footage, timed and without sound. Pretty girls scale cinderblock.
Reverse projection is something I'm inclined to highlight.
Shadow, too—and just a shaft of light.

# 1 ¦ WHAT WE COUNT ON

## TOO MUCH TEXT

Let's begin now with the text: we are on a train—the Orient Express, yes,
can you hear it now? And now the earth,
dust and shine.

One night I walked into a bar
put a nickel into the rock 'n' roll box
and played *I got the key to the highway.*

*Give me one more kiss, Momma, just before I go.* We live with the blues
and then tell stories so we have reasons.
It was the Fourth of July—on a blanket at the high school.
Mom wrapped me in her jacket and said,
*Dad put Baron to sleep today.*

Never mind.
The point is that this can't ever stop. So let's begin with the window again.

We are not on a train—but we can imagine that we are.
My dad and I used to drink together. I was tougher then, back when I drank.
And my dad liked that I could hold my liquor. And we would hear the train
        coming.
The train on this earth,
this dust and shine. I cry all the time now.

I lose each small thing.
This is important. I am not a child, and I remember everything.

# ABDUCTION

There were stories before bed, my father with no book,
my sister's black hair on the pillow.
*And two little girls, just about your age.* A story that unlocks
the back door and jumps right out of the kidnapper's car.
And he tells us that the girls ran—
past the lot behind the movie house, the drive-through
dairy, the small vacant school with no tether balls.

It's my turn to tell this story—
startling as a black bug, shiny as bolt cutters, brittle as a palm frond,
just a fleck of blackness and then none.

This is just nostalgia. I know where the dishes go.
I know how the story turns out:
my sister doesn't jump out at the red light.
How did Father know? Besides, he was a cop.
We ran track. It doesn't matter.

You go for a drink, or reach for the checkbook,
and it moves around in there. Once I found a beetle
in a bite of whitefish. Once there was a snake in the house that matched
the color of the couch.

I want you to imagine shiny black hair,
something stuck in a tooth—a buckle, a shoe, a closet, a room.
Imagine a close-up: underwater, weightless, slowed.
I want to tell the story now:
*And the girls ran into the water.* Past the shape of buckets,
the undertow, the color, the sound, a plane pulling a long fluttering sign.

# SLEIGHT OF HAND

I've fallen for the silt and turkey vultures,
the Thai food and sleeper waves,
Molotov cocktails and polystyrene,
soap flakes and the CIA. The cop yesterday
at a press conference holding up
each moment: *tear gas and battering ram*
and *four black-and-whites in front of 7-Eleven*.
I want his hands that won't shake.

Even though it's just
a choreographed illusion
like a sword passing through a
beautiful woman in a basket.
The trick is her black feathered straps,
her legs roped and spread-eagle.
I'm confessing my love for performance.
I'm collecting mother-of-pearl
and pictures of the sky—each curtsy and canary
a lover's hand I'm holding to a thigh.

How can I not submit to this world?
I lift my torn oyster veil every time.
I take in the body dumps and bookmakers,
the calling cards and ephedrine highs.
I kneel down. I make this vagrant world mine.

## WAS IT BEAUTIFUL?

Here is a subdivision west of Van Nuys Airport.
Here is the spindle I hang from, this world, this head of grain.

Here is a little dot on something so small
but tectonic in origin.

Here are my papers. Here is the world
with hepatitis C and a shadow not unlike a cancer scare.

Here is chicken in a paper bag,
shiny hair falling out of a barrette.

Here is the world with oatmeal in its beard
and smoke on its breath.

Was it beautiful? My world?
The kids on my block played T-ball and Tetris

one accidentally shot a boy in the desert.
We did a good job staying unsentimental.

Was it beautiful? Was it instinct? Commerce?
It was the world.

Here is that holy bone
that connects spine to pelvis.

Here is Eagle Rock. Fireweed
on the side of the freeway. A cul-de-sac guardrail.

The earthquake of '94. We painted our faces
by lantern light, washed in the hot-water heater.

Here is the LAPD, the Rodney King riots.
Here is a crunch of dirty ice, some stolen steaks—

you can buy 'em or not, says the world.
Still, I remake it over and over again.

Here is a six-bed crisis facility, a titanium heart valve,
a castle built out of Popsicle sticks.

# THE FABRIC OF AFTERNOON

I can hear a girl drop
a weighted hook into the river.
I am always looking
for where the river dams up,
for where the railroad tracks
wind past a store with a bell that rings
every time a man walks through the door.
I stand like a smokestack.
I blow at the flies overhead.
This is my childhood.
I do it as much as I can.
The widow with her black parasol
turns the ring on her hand.

## MATCHING TERRY SWEATSUITS

This is not the earthquake of '94, not one of Dad's nights—
Dad too drunk to drive home from the wedding
and all the cousins with boxed wine and lavender bridesmaid dresses.
It's not like that. You are a still form on the sofa,
and the music plays loud and if I hold your arm up
it won't fall. Dad is making margaritas—
it's my birthday, remember, and you hear
that wicked moon and how the dogs know
there is a man in a hood, an Iranian man,
no the neighbor, no the day workers, at the door.

We are falling down a hole.
Like when you were lost in the snow that winter. We made pairs
and called your name all afternoon. It was so cold
and Mom blamed somebody—the cabin owner or Dad's laugh—
and there was your hole, wet with snowmelt
and it's not like when we found you quietly there.
Our hands are holding onto each other's matching terry sweatsuits—
green, remember—I didn't want mine, and we could have been so close.

# TO OBSCURE A BODY OF LIGHT

How the girls love to believe
in celestial bodies, in summer
and ice, in bright disks of light.
The abductor is a human creature.

The creature burns like a star
raging white, a constant light,
the girls' dark hair parted to the side.
A young girl disappears—

not in parts, not as night.
The problem is not absence,
but a blinding summer light.
The girls like dark rail ties

set down on dust so bright.
The abductor winds to a stop
with a pistol in his lap. Imagine
such a wreck. Not the act,

but the smell of gasoline.
Not the shape, but a glare
blazing without meaning.
How the girls' bodies grow

longer and darker as the earth
rotates toward twilight.
The orange ball falling
below the horizon line.

How the girls love to believe
in night—even in the white of his eyes,
the whine of his machine,
a single face illuminated by dash-light.

## MY AUNT BELIEVES IN HORSES

My young aunt's hair is falling
into piles of dust from the living.

Her legs bent in a V,
she scatters

her pink cancer pills
over the floorboards.

The pills tell a story of medicine
my aunt no longer believes.

I kneel below her—
just loose flowers

placed in rows,
her body like a holiday float

instead of a woman.
After she dies, my father

places two pictures side by side.
In one, a boy combs each tangle

from my aunt's tough child-hair.
In the other,

the old boy combs
and combs,

his tears falling
like the beautiful

lost hair we sweep
into piles. Like the sound of wind

through eucalyptus trees,
my young aunt's pills have rolled

to each corner of the room.
My father is still gathering them,

even with the late-summer fire
sending the horses galloping

to the edge of a field
behind this suburban street.

\*\*


This is the dust of the living:
Piles on a floorboard.

Stories of medicine. A parade
of timekeeping and intelligence.

I keep marching. I tell stories
my beautiful young aunt

no longer believes—
pictures we place side by side.

I kneel below
the arrangements

we eventually
sweep into piles.

I sweep and sweep.
But the eucalyptus leaves

keep blowing in
through an open window

and my father is sending me
to gather the horses.

**

Outside, all is dust.
But the horses

keep galloping.
The beautiful dusk

of the living
is falling over me.

I chase the horses
who have never believed

in anything
but fire.

\*\*

This suburban street. My legs
bent in a V. I scatter

the stories in which
we no longer believe.

This body has grown so large,
but I am the awkward

woman who is small inside.
Two pictures side by side. A body

I make into a pile
at the edge of this field.

I am listening for my aunt
through the eucalyptus leaves—

a sweep, even a breath
of her living. I will mother

even the smallest fire.
I'll send the stories galloping.

## WHAT WE COUNT ON

A little blood, a little overexposure,
a sunny backyard, some grief.

I'm looking for something—
tender, a pink heating pad, god, a dark juice. This thirst.

I polish my cracked boots,
pick red peppers and eggplant from the vine,

lost again

in a dark wind moving through the yard.

Blackberries drop off every summer, and that terrible wind
spooks the horses.

I know that one day
I will be taken.

Devastated by
the fifty good acres between me
and all that I didn't do.

Oh god, I am sincere.
Like the sound of a thousand ships' masts blowing. Like fabric and fire.

# MY BURGHER DOLLHOUSE

This is the ladder.
This is the latch.
This is the night
I fill the cabinet.

With tiny incisors,
pearls for knobs,
silver crescents
for nail beds—

a dark ladder
of memory scraps.
Like mothering or eating,
I've grown adept

at salvaging. This is my wagon.
This is my scaffolding—
my sheepskin and pork tin.
My memory arcade

of lace, pots, miniature lots—
of crying and omelets.
This is my cabinet,
kindling of unmet need—

of overmothering
and undereating,
my teacup throat
still screaming.

This is the ladder.
This is the latch.
This, the cabinet
I doused with gas.

## 2 ¦ THE PARTING

# THE FACTS

On Highlander Street
In the San Fernando Valley
At about 2:15
A white man in a Ford
Slows to the young female teen
Pulls his gun
Get the fuck in the car
Drives to the back of a locked-up auto repair
Makes her suck his dick
With his gun to her head
Drops her off at Ralph's
With two quarters in her hand

## SNAPSHOT, 1993

I'm holding my sister's cuff,
the hemmed edge of the sleeve
I imagine she wore
as she opens the door
of the kidnapper's hard white truck.
From deep inside,
I don't see the rise
of her new life. Does she survive?
Will she ever drive at night?
My sister and I sit on the sofa,
our heads silent as smoke.
I didn't comb grass from her hair
like I would in some stupid poem.
No. My sister, her sweater
pulled over her knees,
is picking off her own imaginary
black blood, hardened
on the small of the ankle.

# THE SETTING

In the backyard,
each summer,
    the two of us
    sleeping.

Behind the house, a ravine.
    Behind the house, mustard and gypsum weed

weave through the hinges
of an abandoned car's wrecked metal frame.

The chaparral always burning.

The two of us imagining
the car's charred frame—fire consuming

human hair, a paper bag,
an empty bottle turned black.

    After watching *Nightmare on Elm Street,*

I made my sister
curl in bed with me. Each night,
her body wrapped around me.

Like the earth—
not dangerous, but sustaining.

*Do it again, Daddy!*

was the game. When Dad pretended to be mean.
When he pretended to be that face

you can't believe you finally see.

The land, dry
and always burning.

The night my mom and dad
stood watching—

a blaze so loud they couldn't hear our screams.
          But finally, the outline of hair, the sirens blaring.

Someone was coming.

All this retracing and guessing.
My sister and I
          hopped chain-link.

Ran straight into the ravine.
Was the car a fossil? The fire, foreshadowing?

We couldn't wait to see.

# HOW TO UNMAKE A FATHER

Use two parts Bushmills,
one part water. Use a full-grown
fu manchu. *Lie down, Daddy.*
Rub his feet. Take his Richard
Pryor cassettes, the *Rambo* VHS.
Hide the medals from his armoire.
Climb into his electric Chevy.
Make a slit in the tint,
get him to drop his clean rifle
out the car window.

Squeeze his hand-grip
to make your fingers strong.
Know which stolen luggage
belongs to him. If you follow him
like a cop on a vice beat,
you'll know where Daddy goes.
You'll know he's got a wink
just for you—a lean and a laugh
that's half humiliated,
half moonshine.

## THE PARTING

The street echoes nothing
but the muffled steps
of two girls leaving
*The Rocky Horror Picture Show.*
Not a car, not the sound
of their slippered feet. The tip
of the girls' lit cigarettes,
the blink and tick of a turn signal
as a truck appears and slows to a crawl.
Some face, a jaw,
two eyes like fish,
falls on the girls
where they last meet.
So scared are the girls
at the signal where each
will go her separate way
and climb back quietly
into her bedroom window.
Such a small girl
who begs the tall girl
to please please
walk her home.

## MAKE-BELIEVE WITH THE LAPD

*One, two, three, four*
is how we timed

how fast my sister and I
could find night—

how fast we'd outrun
your big hands,

the tough cords
of our backs

heaving inside
the dark garage

full of rifles
and gasoline, the three of us

laughing.
You were our playtime

intruder, your dark
vice-cop curls, your fu manchu.

It was a game, a training.
*Are you afraid of the dark?*

you'd say. I'm seven and
inside your arms.

When they combed
my sister for samples,

her jacket and pubic hair—
her shoes, her cuffs,

under her fingernails.
*Step outside the car,*

you say, before coming in
off the night shift

with men and instructions,
buzzing up through a radio.

You, chewing a toothpick
in the passenger seat

of a black-and-white.
Even you couldn't stop

what nobody
sees coming.

You're calling in a plate number,
so tired of this business

rising out of static.

## SEDNA BECOMES INUIT GODDESS
## OF THE SEA: A PREQUEL

A seabird has promised you
a stinking nest of bearskins and fish.
You have no choice in who you love.
If you try to leave, Father will put you in a canoe,
shove you overboard. He will cut your fingers
if you hold onto the lip; he will smack you
with his oar. Live for him: on old fish food,
and what you can make from your fingers.
When your hands ache, don't punish
the carp and hagfish with sickness and storms.
Live on for him: in your house of whale rib and
ground, your one good leg always bent beneath
a cauldron of boiling seals.
Old woman, forgive the sea,
let the people starve.

# HUM

Think of insects: the simple eyes and antennae, the hard spiracles
of the abdomen. The lives of some insects are so short they last
only one day.
Segmented creatures—
a well-defined head and three pairs of legs.

Mom wants to move her alcoholic brother out of his pickup truck
somewhere along the border of Arizona
into her new upstairs spare bedroom. Life is painful, she tells me.

Of course I know life is painful—
full of unfair hints and secrets. I begin to think of people who eat raw
seeds and day-old bread. They wander, wrapping themselves
in someone's lost clothing, pulling bags and carts of yesterday's newspapers.
Mom wants to save them, too. I think they might be okay out there,
collecting all our forgotten spangles.

Insects can eat fabric, opium, cork, and tobacco. They keep
the plums and carrots clean and can live inside fields of clover and alfalfa.

I listen for their hum in the clover—
for the dark-blue shades of twilight, for truant schoolgirls
lighting their first cigarettes. Every day there are shadows
from other celestial bodies passing over earth,
there are queen honeybees laying eggs, unspent work furloughs
and silver fish hatching at the mouth of some cool river.

# THE MYTHS

When El Niño comes, the water drags
raccoons and possums,     an old Datsun

parked in the Sepulveda Basin.
    The flooding
makes the hard land
come out from under stucco houses

and into the concrete wash
my neighbor ran alongside for two miles—

    the dead boy and his bike
floating inside.

LA's own great flood.
Not only as folklore, but seventeen days of rain

and a thirty-foot mound of mud
    that buries sixteen homes.

We dig shells and fish fossils
from the desert floor,
    dream of earthquakes and tsunamis
scoring clay, coast,

the weight of earth to ocean.

Weather as myth.
Weather as the story

of dust on a canyon floor.
Like our ancestors' own great deluge—
    taking families and crops,

sent by the gods to purify civilization.

Scholars now say those floods were just
small, local events.

But for the villagers

the river kept on rising and rising.

    They clung
to their tools and their stories
as water covered every part of their known world.

## SNAPSHOT, 1982

There's a glowing light
just beyond the property line.
Inside the house,
two twin beds,
two plastic pink phones
strung from room to room.
Every summer, the fires
chase the horses.
They come galloping
up the concrete.
The pink phone buzzing.
My little unicorn clock.
My little music box. My sister
knock knocking
on the other side
of the plaster wall.

## ANTI-ELEGY

There's no metaphor, no PIN number,
no point of accumulation

where I'll ever stop measuring
the loot I'm piling up

on a little blanket in my mind.
I'm holding on to my duties

like a stack of bills, a cache—
this empty till.

Girls are combing their hair into thick ponytails.
You don't get to keep any of it.

## MY SISTER

My sister's eyes     shimmer like gold&blue streetlights

flickering in the wind at night     hair black like Cherokee

like wrens nesting in eaves     like hoodoo flim-flam

a thoroughbred     my sister the butcher a hatchet man

her every cell blazing     racing through palm groves

naked as a belly     an outrigger with timber back

out of my sister's mouth     a crown of threaded seeds

my sister the poplar the swallow     a jar hanging from a tree

outbreaks like a broken-down RV     tick-tock tick-tock tick-tock

my sister the fodder     villagers bind into sheaves

# WINTER

Bent inside a small kitchen,
a man pulls rubbish from the bin.
It's Sunday. The geese wait
outside for dark beans
and soft romaine. He's folded
each dish towel into a pile
from gray to green.
Art so simple and necessary.
A life so tidy. His wash bin.
His one dish of cream.
Out on the frozen lake,
the loud white geese
signal his arrival.
The rotten lettuce falls
to the ice. He likes the
geese to look proud.

Elemental seems
the world, the ice—
a story of a man
who touches only
geese with his hands.
The snow, the row,
the vegetables—each detail
ordered. Whatever's
concealed, whatever doesn't fit,
stays quiet and cold.
In my mind, I pile equipment
under a tarp for winter rain—

objects to build a story
like a single straight line
through time: *When I was child.*
*I could smell peat moss.*
*Under the strain*
*of earth.*

I draw lines with a stick
in the snow. The old man stands,
the cup of his palm,
such a tiny space for feeling,
empty again. The world
is elemental—
not art, not a story that reads:
I'm alone. I'm alone.
And the old man,
the kitchen, the bin—
just an invention.
I'm out on this lake,
freezing.

## DIVIDED HIGHWAY

Over this asphalt, I let each cactus,
each unfolding mile of dust, each pole,

each turning worry—become ash and light
through a wide glass windshield.

I am not a barn owl or Torrey pine. I'm not the crows
or candy wrappers flying. I'm not going home to get my rifle.

I'm singing. My song is like laundry blowing
on a line. Here I am! Here I am!

I'm driving eighty-five. I'm eating bacon again.
I'm not slowed by the high speeds at which we race

toward that final dark suit, not just pressed and clean
but patiently waiting. I hold onto the steering wheel.

I know exactly where I'm going.

# 3 ¦ LATCHKEY

# BLACKTOP GIRLS

The girls pile into a Chevy and swoosh through a quiet night,
kissing each other and holding tight to that straight gold line
in the middle of the highway, the smell of wet ragweed
and malt liquor, the night entering each girl
like dark dye blossoming in water. Night after night
the girls pull stickers from each other's hair,
sing to an old darkness, to a life that waits for them
like some slick gentleman lighting matches under a streetlight.
He lifts a heavy backpack from one girl's shoulders,
tucks the other girl's hair away from her eyes.
The girls race toward him like an ambulance,
the body waving *good-bye, good-bye.* The girls whispering
*I love you* into the night—as if the body knows only beauty,
as if the body isn't a stacked truck lumbering out of sight.

## BLUE BALLS, REVISED

I wanted my first time to be like that scene in *Don't Look Back*
when Dylan plays "It's All Over Now, Baby Blue"
and Donovan just looks at him. But I'd have to
revise the summer I turned fourteen.

In the new version, there's a circle of boys.
My guy's a firecracker, a bet, a smack. He's my
liquor cabinet. My close smell.
A place my legs get to wrap.

In the new version, I won't chicken out.
I won't shave my head, puke off my skateboard,
watch *Saturday Night Live* on acid.

I didn't want to be a girl anymore.
Not after I finally let him roll me over,
months later, and just a little blood. I'd cut what he said
to his friends about my little cup, my bed, me never speaking.
Twenty years later I still think sex

is something tough, a breaking.
So in this version, I get to be Dylan. I get to drop
into an empty pool—the sound of my skateboard,
my can of Michelob, and I'm never afraid.

## AT REHAB

Now you're looking up at this circle of faces:
a washed-up boxer, the guy scarred from third-degree meth burns,
the seventy-pound benzodiazepine addict leaning on a cane,
the girl locked in her aunt's closet until she was five.
You hear the staff fridge humming. You tap a cigarette.

It's "group": they say you're a runner, a shutdown, in denial, turned off, standoffish.
*You've got Cadillac problems,* they say.
At night, when the lights go, you think of home,
the chickens and half-empty cans of latex paint.

The rules are: no fighting, fucking, or fruit from the trees.
Finally, you crack—not because of them or even the one detail
your sister remembers after that man kidnapped her, gave her change.

But because you want to get high.
You want the human species to reach its K line—
how happy you were when that science teacher told you humans
should reproduce like elephants but instead do it like pond scum.

At rehab, you all line up together for cheese sandwiches,
can openers, nightly meds. You tap a cigarette—
it's double scrub. You get the wet mop
while your roommate's stuffing toilet paper and Ajax into a plastic water bottle.
*It's a vinegar bomb,* she says, *we just need some vinegar*—you get a boost,
grab a lemon, toss it to her, so you can watch the thing explode.

# THE POWERFUL

Who can blame the strippers in the Valley—
    inverted, ankles hooked over a silver pole,
shining
    like a lubricated nine-millimeter securing a field of gazes.
I want to be able to do what my father did with his gun.

I want to not only live in the world,
but become powerful enough
to shape it out of its dream, its ambiguity—
the earth turning to mud beneath our feet,
    El Niño drowning a boy and his bike
    in the LA River.

I understand my dad and his cop friends—
after coming home from Vietnam,
and so many fatal crashes on the 101.
    *Ground beef on asphalt,* they'd say.
    Or hog-tie a man upside down
    from the door of a freshly waxed police car.

# WHAT WE LEARN AT VALLEY HIGH

The PE coaches teach us about sex.
They corner me if a top is unzipped.
They watch me spray Aqua Net into my bangs.
We can always jump for them, or hit the loading-dock fences
and ditch sixth period for burgers and bong loads.

Kurt Cobain isn't dead yet,
but we light fires for him during Spanish class.
We're learning which little deaths come next.
We're doing whip-its in a truck before first period.
Rebecca is puking in the F Building toilet—her dad in jail
for molesting her best friend. There's a fight on the quad.
I'm holding onto my boyfriend's wallet chain.

I'm walking into a kegger in Box Canyon:
Manson's cave, with an Indian face carved into sandstone,
looks down at us. I'm stepping out of a green Chevelle,
zipping up my pants. Phil is jumping off a roof after selling
bathtub speed to twelve-year-olds. I can't see.

Ten guys beat a man who cornered two girls
in a vacant house next door. They piss on him afterwards.
They make his right eye blind. When we come home,
Lisa's mom is catching rain from her leaky roof into cookie sheets.
*Is he dead?* she asks. Each of us falls onto a couch.
There's the sound of drops hitting metal.

## CALIFORNIA PITH

We thought we could fly away:
sixteen-year-old arms hanging out a car window,
the future as far away as a firing squad
in another century
buried in a textbook
at the bottom of a locker.

We thought we could slow the world down
so it moved like a violin solo—
the way our being high made the billboards and cars
seem far enough from the windows,
and from those essential bonelike parts of ourselves,
the very structures that seemed to hold us up.

And because of this slowness
our voices would rise inside the car
in worship of the single moment—
singing and spoiled and sick
and veering over the center divider.

Fashion was an identity then,
a long coat with fur around the collar, a red striped
flea market tee, some skinny girl's sad story
we draped over ourselves.
No one escapes the world's marks—
the edits that refine each story.

Even now, I think of the way the California sun
changes each fall

and that car we all rode in down the 101,
though we weren't really children—
and our hair is long again
and the hills along the freeway open up to the ocean
so steady and lost
in a motion that goes on forever.

It's such a thin moment
when I look in the rearview mirror and
we're sinking and singing and I keep on driving.

## THE NIGHT STALKER

In the summer of 1984, Richard Ramirez wandered
through our well-kept yards, raping and killing
old women in their condos and Toyotas—
some neighbor's chain-link gate hanging wide open.
Julie's mom counted out her pills
and set a plastic plate of tuna sandwiches
under the streetlights where we played.
Julie's broken strand of pearls,
her fingers pressed against my lips,
a game we played on some stupid
Parker Brothers Ouija board.

No intruder jimmied off a screen while Julie
pretended the ghost inside her
made her molest each girl,
one by one, like the rows of
post–World War II houses we hid inside.
A game she learned behind a wet bar
in some vet's spare bedroom.
So that each time she pinched a thigh
or let the girl down the street ring her doorbell
while she hid one of us under the dining room table,
we became her stunned dolls—
hard black eyes and a stitched line for a smile.

Each girl feared that Night Stalker
who crawled into a kitchen every night
on the eleven o'clock news—
a dishwasher still sloshing,

our nail polish and ballet slippers, a closet door
sliding open and closed, Julie's hands teaching
us what she was taught. For years, all of us
with Julie in some man's bed.
A concrete wall at the end of each property—
little families moving from room to room.

## IN HUMBOLDT COUNTY

I owed my dealer money
for every pinched ounce

but made up for it
with the four grown men

sleeping on the floorboards
of our all-girl house.

Elijah made rattles out of seaweed
and Dominique could heal his own sight

with psilocybin and ecstasy.
I'd come to at any moment

with a dick in my back,
or an all-night jimbay jam,

or a roommate trading hash
for food stamps. Every paper recycled,

every scrap composted,
every bar of soap

quartered into shares—
we don't shake or shave

in Humboldt County;
we cough and grow pot

and tend tree forts
built for a draft dodge.

Nelly and Bug
let their boy's nose run

while we puffed on
glass-blown chillums

and my roommates said,
how dare I work for a big logger

who warmed his truck
and left each night

for AA meetings,
his boys seven and nine,

their mom dead from AIDS—
and all I had to do

was get them in
a school bus on time.

## HOW GENTLY THE WORDS
## HAVE BEEN PLACED INTO MY MOUTH

I'm a girl who has burned
something like enamel
not onto my toenails, not *tea-shell cream* or
*turquoise-dream,* but on a surface
that's almost me.
Do you know what this means?
*I just want to touch.*
But the signs tell me a girl
better dream she's soft with love.
Voilà! I love my work boots.
I love this parcel hoop, this pinafore
and the rain after four.
I love kissing
my practice-hopes.
Like I actually believe.
It's okay. The world is man-made.
I won't split my chin.
I'll pull along this wagon
of oysters and omelets, monks
and Nat King Cole.
I can make *hand*
equal the cup
of a gorilla's palm.
Sure, it's black, clumsy,
heavier than the trunk
of an elephant.
But I can make a train
from tin cans. A mother

from seventeenth-century sheepskin.
I'll make a deck of cards
from woodcuts of Charles the VI.
One for each player.
A Spade from Italian suits.
Don't leave me.
I'm a farmhand.
Not rich.
But I can grow delicate again.
I'll make glass sandals.
I'll place the coin in the hand of the ferryman.

# NERVE

Here are the wandering vagrants:

myself, my sister, my mother and father

connected by heart rate, sweat, brain stem.

Our plane rocks and my abdomen opens

to a history of blows. My dad cracks

a beer and I unclick the belt to cry

in the small plastic bathroom.

No one is at home in a body

that kicks back. Some great nerve

that connects cranium to abdomen.

The heaviness of memory, repeated blows

after the blows have stopped.

The four of us sit quietly like panhandlers

in a row. We beg to be full.

# FORGIVENESS

In a room with a ticking clock

a man with Agent Orange bumps on his back

a woman in soft nightclothes

in chronic disk pain

a child clutching her stomach

each silent creature

bowing the head for grace

unmerited.

# ADDICTION

It starts with a sugared gruel, a colostrum
for your aching pores. You want to know
what everyone is laughing about.
You're all salmon on the inside.
You get addicted to the act
of saving yourself. First
the saliva. Then each hair
in each follicle. A fix.
The shakes. A brightness.
A clicking in your ear.
You've been pegged
all along. Your hands
are where they can see 'em.
They're searching your face,
your plate numbers,
your glove box.
You're addicted
to that straight stare
into the distance.

# ELEPHANT GIRL

The beast is twirling
to the light
in someone else's eyes—
such a small pedestal,
such purpose.
Like a Doberman pinscher,
Elephant Girl
believes in a strength
that has grown
into something
like her own rough, stiff hair.
Go on, touch the long trunk.
Her belly is no mother,
no grassy space
between you and your
undiscovered beauty.
She is spinning
on her fat foot sole.
She has grown so tranquilized.

## SNAPSHOT, 1978

In the photograph,
her face is turned toward
the flash of the bulb.
There's the little velvet dresses,
tinsel on a tree.
Outside the frame,
someone's blending ice
for eggnog. There's no snow,
no ash, no graphic details,
no pharmaceuticals.
Our red Christmas dresses.
The camera's glare.
My sister's beautiful
dumb face.

# LATCHKEY

Catholics, liars, cops,
a pocket of pills,

a hard plastic doll.
I might have been a fat child.

I might have taken scissors
to my own red hair.

Not fine, but loaded on Dr. Pepper
and too much free time.

No one told me what I love
doesn't have to be ugly.

I've borrowed this tuxedo,
this top hat. I make jazz hands.

I've learned tap. On the closed-circuit
TV in my mind,

I kneel down.
The surveillance footage is in black and white,

timed and without sound.
I've grown sick of listening

for coyotes and house cats—
through all the commuter traffic,

through the blaring ACs.
I'm out and I want to come in free.

# OUTER SPACE

Each of us like a little light saber

with a Force that could bind
not just the world,

but the entire galaxy together.

We believed in Science Fiction,
in nuclear ballistic missiles, X-ray technology,
     Ronald Reagan's big red button.
We loved the slender whiteness
     of our plastic rocket boosters.

We watched the Challenger explode
on a forty-inch TV the yard-duty
rolled into our classroom.

First, liftoff
     and that long plume of smoke—
before the announcement over the PA system:
*Schoolchildren of America . . .*
*man's horizons . . .*
*the crew's final mission . . .*

And each kid
went home to small plastic toys
while the world went on about O-rings
     and washed-up debris.

As it turns out, space
    just keeps on expanding and accelerating—

made up of a dark energy that one day
will rip our gravity away.

So we took the railroad tracks to the park by the wash
    and climbed to the top

of the metal rocket slide.

We can't not look up at those stars—

even if they are    just gas    and dust    swirling
from a freezing stellar wind.

    We're waiting for transmission
in a wave of silence,

our bodies like little signal towers,
    our hoods pulled over our heads.

# COME BRIGHT GALAXY

*For Annie Blue*

Out of static, not fluid,
her heartbeat rises through the audible wool of space.

There's a quickening.
There's the rain—on the tin, on the timber world.

Her cells explode like tiny
golden kites popping over a dark cow pasture.

Bright scraps for our epic.
I'm waiting for the world to light up.

Luminosity isn't just warmth
or opened light, but a body of heat tethered to earth

by gravity, which is ordinary.
A woman will stare into pale strands of observable light—

but this is delicate moss,
a simple swelling. The body is a work song.

We are returning
to this ordinary and dear world: these tiny blue flowers,

this standard sediment.

## ACKNOWLEDGMENTS

Thank you to the editors of the following publications, in which these poems originally appeared:

"Matching Terry Sweatsuits," formerly "You Are Still Faced," *5am;*

"Too Much Text," "How to Unmake a Father," "Blue Balls, Revised," "What We Learn at Valley High," "Make-Believe with the LAPD," "Snapshot, 1978," "Snapshot 1982," "Snapshot, 1993," "In Humboldt County," "Addiction," and "At Rehab," *Askew;*

"Sedna Becomes Inuit Goddess of the Sea: A Prequel," *The Bedside Guide to No Tell Motel;*

"My Aunt Believes in Horses," *Los Angeles Review;*

"Blacktop Girls," "Divided Highway," and "Sleight of Hand," *MiPOesias;*

"To Obscure a Body of Light," "The Setting," "The Parting," "Outer Space," and "My Burgher Dollhouse," *No Tell Motel;*

"What We Count On," *Pool;*

"Was It Beautiful?" and "Abduction," *Pebble Lake Review;*

"Winter," *Scribbler;*

"Hum," *Solo: A Journal of Poetry;*

and "California Pith," *Tar River Poetry.*

"Abduction" was nominated for a Pushcart Prize. "Hum" was reprinted in *Blue Arc West: An Anthology of California Poetry.* A portion of this manuscript was published as a limited-edition chapbook titled *Divided Highway* (Dancing Girl Press, 2008).

I'd also like to gratefully acknowledge the guidance, encouragement, and support of my teachers—especially Dorothy Barresi, Amy Gerstler, Leilani Hall, Ed Ochester, and Jill Waldron.

Thanks, also, to Sandra Hunter, Marsha De la O, Phil Taggart, and Jackson Wheeler—for their tireless work in the service of poetry. Thank you to my writing group crew and to all my friends who've believed in my poetry. This book wouldn't have made its way into the world if it weren't for the wise counsel of Lee McCarthy and Joan Raymond, both of whom have passed on.

Finally, I'd like to acknowledge my family—my mother, father, and sister—for bravely standing behind this project. And to my husband, Jeff, and our daughter, Annie Blue—on our pirate ship.